... of CAMBRIDGE
...minations

Top Tips for FCE

Acknowledgements

Cambridge ESOL is grateful to the following author and publisher for permission to reproduce copyright material in the text:

Little, Brown Book Group for the adapted text on pages 14 and 15 from *A Case to Answer* by Margaret Yorke © Little, Brown Book Group.

Every effort has been made to identify the copyright owners for material used, but it has not always been possible to identify the source or contact the copyright holders. In such cases, Cambridge ESOL would welcome information from the copyright owners.

For permission to reproduce photographs:

Corbis for p. 50, pp. 54–55
Getty Images for pp. 54–55 (parking ticket)
Ark Creative for pp. 54–55 (tickets)

Cambridge ESOL would also like to thank the following for their contributions to this project: Petrina Cliff, Heather Daldry, Helen Naylor, Jacky Newbrook, Felicity O'Dell and Brian Orpet.

University of Cambridge ESOL Examinations
1 Hills Road, Cambridge, CB1 2EU, UK
www.CambridgeESOL.org

© UCLES 2008

First published 2008
Printed in the United Kingdom by Cambridge Printing Services Ltd

ISBN: 978-1-906438-25-8

Contents

Introduction

Top Tips for FCE is an essential part of your revision for the First Certificate in English (FCE), the B2-level exam from Cambridge ESOL. Each of the five main chapters (Reading, Writing, Use of English, Listening and Speaking) follows the same structure and is based on a series of pieces of advice (the 'tips') which examiners have collected from many years' experience of setting and marking FCE papers.

Each section usually starts with a tip at the top of the page. The tip is followed by an example taken from real FCE material and a clear explanation to help you understand exactly what it means.

Each chapter ends with some more 'General tips' for that paper. There is also a handy section at the beginning of the book on how to revise for FCE and a very important section at the back on what you should do on the day of the exam.

How to use Top Tips for FCE

Take the *Top Tips for FCE* book with you and read it when you have a few minutes during the day. Then use the CD-ROM to practise at home: it contains a real FCE exam paper for you to try, together with the answers for Reading, Use of English and Listening and some sample student answers for the Writing paper. The CD-ROM also includes all the recordings for the Listening paper and a video of real students doing an FCE Speaking test, to show you exactly what you will have to do when you take the test. Practise with some classmates using the Speaking test material on the CD-ROM and compare your performance with the students on the video.

Top Tips for FCE is flexible. You can look at a different tip from a different paper every day, or you can start at the beginning with the tips for the Reading paper and work through until you get to the end of the tips for the Speaking test. Whichever method you prefer, read the example and the explanation carefully to make sure that you understand each tip. When you have understood all the tips for each paper, try the real exam paper on the CD-ROM.

Guide to symbols

 This symbol introduces the 'tip' which is usually at the top of the page. Each tip is some useful advice to help you find the right answer for Reading, Use of English or Listening. For Writing, the tips show you how to write a better answer to the question, and for Speaking, they explain how you can give good answers which show your true level of English to the examiners.

 This is an extra piece of advice which is important for this particular part of the test.

 This symbol tells you to go to the CD-ROM where you will find a real FCE paper to try.

We hope that *Top Tips for FCE* will help you with your preparation for taking the FCE exam.

Cambridge ESOL

Ho D

Guide to FCE task types

Multiple choice You have to read a text or listen to a recording. Each question has three or four options and you have to decide which the correct answer is. *(Reading: Part 1, Listening: Parts 1 and 4)*

Gapped text A text with some empty spaces (gaps). After the text there are some sentences or paragraphs. You have to choose the correct sentence or paragraph for each gap. *(Reading: Part 2)*

Multiple matching You read a series of questions and a long text or several short texts or you listen to a series of short recordings by different speakers. For each question, you have to decide which text or part of the text, or which speaker mentions this. *(Reading: Part 3 and Listening: Part 3)*

Cloze A text in which there are some missing words or phrases (gaps). There are two types of 'cloze' in the Use of English paper. Part 1 is a multiple-choice cloze task, where you choose the answer from the four options we give you. Part 2 is an open cloze, where you have to think of the right word for the gap.

Word formation A text containing ten gaps. Each gap represents a word. At the end of the line is a 'prompt' word which you have to change in some way to make the correct missing word and complete the sentence correctly. *(Use of English: Part 3)*

Key word transformations A sentence followed by a key word and a second sentence which has a gap in it. You have to use the key word to complete the second sentence so that it means the same as the first sentence. *(Use of English: Part 4)*

Sentence completion A recording with one, two or more speakers lasting approximately 3 minutes. To answer the questions, you have to complete the sentences on the question paper with information you hear on the recording. *(Listening: Part 2)*

Long turn The examiner gives you a pair of photographs to talk about and you have to speak for 1 minute without interruption. *(Speaking: Part 2)*

Collaborative task Conversation with the other candidate. The examiner gives you some pictures and a decision-making task to do. You have to talk with the other candidate and make a decision. *(Speaking: Part 3)*

How to revise for FCE

It is important to use the time that you have to revise for FCE as well as possible. Here are some general ideas to help you do this.

Make a plan!

It is a good idea to make a plan for your last month's study before the exam. Think about:

- what you need to do
- how much time you have
- how you can fit what you need to do into that time.

Try to be realistic when you make your plan. If you plan to do too much, then you may soon be disappointed when you fall behind.

Think about what you need to know!

Remember that FCE is a test of your general level of English. You don't have an exam syllabus listing what information you have to learn as you do in, for example, chemistry or history. So most things that you do in English will help you to improve – reading a story or a newspaper article may be as useful as doing a grammar exercise, for example.

It is important, however, that you know exactly what you will have to do in the exam. Doing some practice papers will help you develop good exam techniques and this will save you time in the exam room. But don't spend all your revision time doing practice papers!

Think about what you need to improve. Ask your English teacher what you need to work on – reading, writing, speaking or listening, grammar or vocabulary.

Look back at homework that your teacher has corrected. What mistakes did you make? Do you understand where you went wrong? What are your weaknesses?

Have what you need to hand!

In order to prepare for FCE you probably need:

- a good learners' dictionary (one with examples of how words are actually used in English)
- an FCE-level coursebook (you are probably using one of these if you do regular classes)
- some examples of FCE papers
- a vocabulary notebook
- notes or other materials from your English course (if you are doing one)
- a bilingual dictionary
- a good grammar book.

If you have easy access to a computer you can get some of these online – the dictionaries and the examples of FCE papers, for instance.

Also have a good supply of stationery such as pens, pencils, highlighters and paper. Some students find it convenient to write things like vocabulary on cards, which they can then carry with them and look at when they have a spare moment on the bus or in a café.

Think about when and where you study!

Most people find it best to study at regular times at a desk with a good light and everything they need beside them.

Some people find they work best in the early mornings, while others prefer the evenings. If possible, do the main part of your revision at the time of day which is best for you.

However, you may also find that there are other good times and places for you to study. Perhaps when you are making a meal or doing some housework you could listen to some English on an mp3 player. Or you could read something on your way to work or school.

Organise your revision time well!

Allow time for breaks when you are revising – many students like to study for an hour and a half, for example, and then have a half-hour break.

Vary what you do – sometimes focus on listening, sometimes on vocabulary, sometimes on writing. This will make sure that you don't neglect any aspect of the language and will also make your revision more interesting.

It is sensible to do something completely different before you go to bed – go for a walk, have a bath, read a relaxing book or watch a favourite film.

Enjoy your revision!

Find some enjoyable activities that help your English – listen to songs in English or watch TV or some English-language DVDs.

What do you like doing in your free time? Could you combine that with English practice too? For example, if you like a particular sport or singer or if you are interested in the news or computer games, you should easily be able to find something in English about your interest on the internet.

Revise with a friend – you can practise talking to each other in English and can perhaps help each other with any questions you have.

Keep fit!

Don't forget that feeling fit and healthy will help you get good marks too:

- make sure you get plenty of sleep
- remember to eat sensibly
- take some exercise.

Now here are some ideas to help you organise your revision for the individual papers in FCE.

Paper 1: Reading

The more you read in English before the exam, the better you will do in this paper. Reading is probably the best way to improve your grammar and vocabulary.

You will learn most if you enjoy what you are reading. So don't choose something that is too difficult for you. Remember that it doesn't have to be serious – unless, of course, you prefer serious things. There are lots of different students who have enjoyed each of these types of reading:

- newspaper articles
- sports magazines
- film reviews
- romantic stories
- children's stories
- travel information – about your own country or a place you have been to
- translations of books you have already read in your own language
- graded readers (well-known books which are adapted to your level of English).

Don't look up every word in a dictionary when you read as this will spoil your pleasure in reading. Just look up anything that is essential for understanding. Then when you have finished you can go back and look up some more words and make a note of any useful expressions from the text.

Keep a reading diary – write a couple of sentences in English about what you have read. This should help you to use some of the language from what you have read. It will also help you with the Writing paper.

Paper 2: Writing

For this paper, it is important to practise writing regularly in English.

- Use some of the new vocabulary and expressions that you have learned from your reading.

- If possible ask a teacher or native English speaker to correct your work. Ask them to correct your mistakes and also to suggest a more interesting way of expressing what you want to say.
- Listen carefully to their advice and use it in the next piece of writing that you do.

Paper 3: Use of English

This is the paper where doing practice tests may help you most. However, you also need to have a good control of grammar and vocabulary to do well.

- So, do some extra practice with materials which focus on grammar and vocabulary (your teacher may be able to advise you which books are best).
- Research shows that you learn best when you write or talk about things that are important to you. So practise making sentences about your own life and experience using structures or vocabulary that you want to learn.
- When you read or listen to English, think about the language that the writer or speaker is using and pay attention to the way that they combine words.

Paper 4: Listening

Even if you are a long way from an English-speaking country, it is possible to practise listening to English. For example, there are lots of things you can listen to on the internet.

- Listen to the news in English on the radio or on an English-language TV channel as much as possible.
- Watch DVDs of English-language films. You may be able to watch a film with subtitles. This can make listening easier and more enjoyable and will help to give you confidence in listening to English.
- Try watching a film in English that you have already seen in your own language.
- Listening to songs in English can be an enjoyable and relaxing way of listening to English. It is often possible to find the words for songs on the internet.

Paper 5: Speaking

Make the effort to practise speaking English whenever you can.

- Get together with friends and agree that you will speak only English for half an hour.
- Join an English language club if there is one in your area.
- Try to make contact with English speakers visiting your area. Perhaps you could get a little work as a tour guide.
- If there are students whose first language is English in your area, try to arrange to exchange conversation sessions with them. (You talk for half an hour in your language and half an hour in English.)
- When listening to English-language films or television, think about the language that the speakers use and, where possible, make use of it when you are speaking yourself.
- Make sure that you can talk about yourself, give opinions, ask someone to repeat or explain, agree and disagree. You may need to do all of these things in the exam.

We hope these ideas will help you to make the most of your revision time. Above all, we hope that you enjoy your studies and wish you all the very best for the exam.

Paper 1: Reading

What's in the Reading paper?

Part 1 ⓠ 8 multiple-choice questions
☑ 2 marks for each correct answer

Part 2 ⓠ gapped text with 7 questions
☑ 2 marks for each correct answer

Part 3 ⓠ text with 15 multiple-matching questions
☑ 1 mark for each correct answer

🕐 **1 hour**

Reading: Part 1 multiple choice

TIP: If you replace pronouns in the options (A, B, C or D) with the nouns they refer to in the text, it is easier to see the correct answer.

Example

Here is the first paragraph of a Part 1 text taken from a novel, and one of the questions.

> The railway station at Becktham had recently been modernised, its ironwork painted vivid red and blue, even a coffee bar established on the platform for London. Trains carried commuters back and forth, running frequently at peak times and maintaining a good service throughout the day. A number of Granbury's regular travellers found it worth driving the extra miles to use this route rather than the nearer station at Nettington, where the car park was filled to capacity long before the first cheap fares were available at nine o' clock. **Charlotte too found it suited her better, for she hated trying to insert her blue Fiat, small as it was, into the last remaining space which was never quite big enough.**

 Why had Charlotte chosen to travel from Becktham Station rather than Nettington Station?

A Faster trains stopped there.

B There were better facilities there.

C The fare was cheaper from there.

D It was easier to park there.

Explanation: 'There' in the options refers to Becktham. The last sentence **(in bold)** gives you the answer **D** which compares Becktham (there) with Nettington, where parking was more difficult.

Reading: Part 1 multiple choice

TIP: Don't look for the same word in the question and the text. Think of synonyms for words in the options, then choose the option that is closest in meaning to the text.

Example

Here is a paragraph of a Part 1 text taken from a novel, and one of the questions.

She had planned to catch the 9.05, but thought she might not manage it when she arrived at the booking office. A large man in a dark suit was making a complicated booking with his credit card and seemed unaware of the fact that there were other passengers queuing up behind him. Buying his season ticket, Charlotte deduced, **mildly irritated** by the delay **but content** to catch the train due fifteen minutes later, for she had no morning appointment and was planning to visit an art exhibition before meeting Lorna.

 How did Charlotte feel about having to queue for a ticket?

A surprised that waiting was necessary

B anxious about how long it would take

C resigned to missing her train

D cross with herself for not anticipating it

Explanation: The words in **bold** give you the answer. 'Irritated' is another word for 'cross' (Option D). However, Charlotte was 'content' to catch the next train. 'Resigned to' means 'irritated but accepting the situation', so the answer is therefore **C**.

Reading: Part 2 gapped text

TIP: Underline any references ('these', 'they', 'it', etc.) and linking words ('although', 'but', etc.) in both the text and the sentences. Remember that words in the text may refer forwards to something in the missing sentence, or to something in the text before or after the gap.

Example

Here is a paragraph from a Part 2 text called 'The World's Smallest Bird'. The missing sentences are inserted in the correct place.

The World's Smallest Bird

A group of nature photographers go in search of the bee hummingbird.

After years of studying hummingbirds, we can normally spot them in flight.

1 | But when we first encountered the bee hummingbird, buzzing and hovering nearby, even we were fooled into thinking it was an insect.

At an estimated 8 beats per second, the bee hummingbird's wings move so rapidly that the naked eye cannot detect them.

Fortunately, we had come prepared. Included in the 75 kilograms of equipment we were struggling to carry through the swamp were high-speed lights.

2 | Only with these could we capture the birds in action.

Using feeders to attract the birds down from 30-metre high trees, we were able to obtain the first photographic documentation of the species.

Explanation: The words in the green boxes in the example above show you the links between the text and the missing sentences.

Reading: Part 2 gapped text

 TIP: There may be a connection between the text and the missing sentence through vocabulary or topic.

Example

Here is a paragraph from a Part 2 text called 'The World's Smallest Bird'. The missing sentences are inserted in the text.

> 4 | Bee hummingbirds measure a bit more than five centimetres from bill to tail.
>
> However, only the male of the species ranks as the smallest of birds, as the female is slightly longer. Attached to a branch with spiders' webs, their nest is no bigger than a doll's teacup. Its soft lining will hold two eggs smaller than coffee beans.
>
> 5 | Although they are so incredibly small, they have an aggressive side.
>
> Many are fiercely territorial, engaging in spectacular aerial battles against other hummingbirds. Indeed, this side of their nature may have been the reason why the Aztec civilisation named a war god after them.

Explanation: In 4, the topic of the paragraph is the size of the bee hummingbird. 'However' introduces a contrast to the missing sentence. In 5, the topic of the hummingbirds' 'aggressive side' is picked up by the word 'fiercely', in the example of 'aerial battles' and 'war god', which provide a vocabulary connection.

Reading: Part 3 multiple matching

 TIP: Underline key words in the questions. These exact words may not be in the text, so look for paraphrases. There may also be more details given in the text to support the answer.

Example

Here is a text from a Part 3 task about men who have had adventures on mountains, and some of the sentences which match this text.

(Q) Which of the young men

1 was determined to have a good time despite the poor conditions?

2 says he was eager to find peace and quiet?

3 gave someone assistance on the way?

A GRAHAM BROOKS

It was a typical Lake District day, wet and horrible, but I'd decided I'd enjoy myself no matter what. I'd made the effort to break free from my office in London, keen to have a much needed rest from the noise and chaos of city life. So my trip to one of the hills, Scafell Pike, started with me putting on all the wet weather gear I owned at the time. As I climbed, conditions deteriorated further, with the cloud base dropping to valley level. As I reached a high point, there in the mist was a young girl of about 10, looking very wet in her thin jacket and jeans. She'd got separated from a school group. I led her onto the summit, where we came across her party. This was one of my more memorable trips to the Pike. To this day, I've never really seen the view from the top.

Explanation: 'Good time' and 'poor conditions' match 'I'd enjoy myself no matter what' and 'wet and horrible' in the text. The numbers on the right of the text show you which phrases match each question.

Reading: Part 3 multiple matching

 TIP: The information may not come in the same order in the text and the questions.

Example

Here is a text from a Part 3 task about men who have had adventures on mountains, and some of the sentences which match this text.

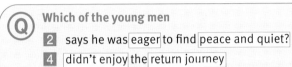

(Q) Which of the young men

2 says he was eager to find peace and quiet?

4 didn't enjoy the return journey

5 seems uninterested in travelling long distances?

B SEAN MURPHY

Looking down over the valley in the Peak District, with a hill across the way and not a sound to be heard other than the breeze in the grass, can really clear your head of the hustle and bustle of a busy week at work, and this is just what I'd come for. I haven't had much opportunity to travel far afield, even in the United Kingdom, but with such beauty on the doorstep, who needs to? I could think of no better way to spend the day than climbing the mountain ahead of me, then down all the way, finishing with a refreshing drink at the Green Dragon Café. Of course, it was a bit of a nuisance having to climb all that way over the same mountain to get back.

Explanation: 'Was eager to find peace and quiet' matches 'just what I'd come for' and 'clear your head of the hustle and bustle of a busy week at work'. The numbers on the right of the text show you which phrases match each question.

Important information may come in different parts of the same sentence.

General tips for Reading

1 Remember to read the instructions for each part first. These will tell you what type of text it is and what it is about.

2 Answer the questions one by one. Don't fill in answers to questions you are uncertain about at first. Cross off those you are sure about as you do them, and go back to those you are unsure of later.

3 Don't just decide which the right answer is. Tell yourself why the others are wrong.

4 Always put an answer on the answer sheet even if you are not totally sure if you are correct.

5 There is always information in the text to help you get the right answer – you never need to guess!

6 In **Part 1,** read the text first without trying to answer any of the questions so that you understand what it is about.

7 In **Part 2,** when you have put all the missing sentences into the text, read the complete text through to check that it makes sense and you can see the links between text and sentence.

8 In **Part 3,** you may not need to read the whole text in detail first. Start by reading the instructions and the questions before you look at the text.

NOW YOU TRY! You will find a complete Reading paper (with answer sheet) to try on the CD-ROM. Give yourself 1 hour to work through the whole paper.

When you have finished you can check your answers.

Paper 2: Writing

What's in the Writing paper?

Part 1 ⓠ 1 compulsory question (120–150 words)
You read some material (up to 160 words) –
advertisements, extracts from letters or emails,
schedules, etc. Then you write a letter or email
using the information in this material.

☑ each question carries equal marks

Part 2 ⓠ 1 question from a choice of 4 (120–180 words),
including an article, email, essay,
letter, report, review and story

☑ each question carries equal marks

🕐 **1 hour 20 minutes**

Your writing is assessed first of all for content. It is then
assessed to see how good the language in your answer
is, considering:

- range of language
- organisation of ideas
- accuracy
- register
- format
- word length

Writing: Part 1

 TIP: Read the instructions carefully. They tell you whom to
write to and why you are writing. There are also notes that
you have to expand. Cross out each note when you have
written about it, but don't copy too much language from
the question.

Example

Here is an example of a Part 1 task. You are planning to visit your
friend Robin in Canada. Read Robin's letter and the notes you have
made on it. Then write a letter to Robin. You must use all your notes.

Great because...

*Say which
and why*

> My friends and I are going to a sports
> camp in the mountains in July. We'd love
> you to join us there. We can play tennis,
> hockey, football and basketball. We can
> stay in rooms or sleep in tents. Which
> would you prefer? We'll cook together in
> the evenings. Is there something special
> from your country that you could cook?
>
> You could fly over to Canada a few days
> before the sports camp and stay with me
> here in the city. What would you like to do
> before we go to camp?

Yes! Explain...

Tell Robin

Explanation: Below are some examples of what you could write to
expand each of the notes.

Great because...
That would be fantastic because I've always
dreamed of going to a sports camp!
Say which and why...
I think I'd rather sleep in a tent because it would
feel much more exciting than sleeping in a room.

Yes! Explain...

I'm afraid I'm not a very good cook, but I could grill some real English sausages for everyone.

Tell Robin...

I'd really love to look round the city and as my village is quite small it would be a really fascinating experience for me.

 TIP: Check your writing when you have finished it, using a checklist like the one below.

Example

Here is an example of a checklist. Use it every time you practise writing something.

Checklist	✔
Have you included all the notes?	
Have you used paragraphs?	
Have you written the right number of words?	
Have you linked the points clearly?	
Have you started sentences in different ways so that it is interesting to read?	
Have you made any mistakes in grammar or spelling?	
Have you used a range of vocabulary? Are there any words you have used too many times?	
Have you started and ended the letter or email correctly?	
Have you used the right style for the person you are writing to?	

Writing: Part 2

TIP: Whichever question you choose to answer, think carefully about the approach you take **before** you start writing.

Example

Here is an example of a Part 2 Writing task.

> You recently took part in a class discussion about choosing an interesting job. Your teacher has now asked you to write an essay, answering the following question and giving reasons for your choice.

 Would you rather be a politician, a teacher or a musician?

Write your **essay**.

Explanation: You could choose to write this essay in three different ways:

1 Choose one job and give reasons why you would choose it.

2 Choose one job and give reasons why you would choose it but also mention negative aspects of the other two jobs.

3 Discuss the positive and negative aspects of all three jobs and say which one you would like to do.

Writing: Part 2

 TIP: When you edit and check your writing, don't only look for grammar and spelling mistakes. Check that you have used an appropriate style for the person you are writing to.

Example

Look at the example of a Part 2 Writing task below.

 Your local tourist office has asked you to write a report for English-speaking visitors giving helpful advice about public transport in your region.

Write your **report**.

Here is an example of a student answer.

Trains

There is a Main Station with good connections to all parts of the region, which is one of the most beautiful in the country, I think. After buying your ticket from the ticket office, it is important to validate it before you get on the train. I forgot once, and an inspector came and I had to pay a fine. I was really angry! There are first class and second class coaches on most trains, and sometimes there is also a restaurant car on long journeys.

Explanation: A report should be written in a neutral style. The highlighted parts of the answer above are too informal and personal.

General tips for Writing

1 Practise writing regularly in English, and always be aware of whom you are writing to, what you are writing for, what style you should be using and what layout is appropriate.

2 Try to use new vocabulary and expressions you have learned.

3 Practise writing things in different ways. This will help to develop your ability to paraphrase, and will also make your writing more interesting.

4 Practise writing using a range of tenses.

5 Remember to plan what you write, and read it through afterwards to check that you have not made any mistakes.

6 When you have finished your answer, check that you have actually answered the question and not included irrelevant details.

7 In **Part 1**, check that you have included all the notes.

8 In **Part 2**, read all the questions carefully before you decide which one to do. Choose to answer the one you feel you are especially good at and you can show your best writing.

 NOW YOU TRY! You will find a complete Writing paper to try on the CD-ROM. Give yourself 1 hour and 20 minutes to work through the whole paper.

When you have finished you can check your answers against the sample answers.

Paper 3: Use of English

What's in the Use of English paper?

Part 1 Ⓠ text with 12 gaps and 4 multiple-choice options for each gap

☑ 1 mark for each correct answer

Part 2 Ⓠ text with 12 gaps

☑ 1 mark for each correct answer

Part 3 Ⓠ text with 10 gaps and the stems of the missing words provided. You change the word to fit the gap

☑ 1 mark for each correct answer

Part 4 Ⓠ 8 separate sentences, each with one sentence and a second sentence with a gap that must be completed using 2–5 words, one of which is the key word

☑ up to 2 marks for each correct answer

🕐 **45 minutes**

Use of English: Part 1 multiple-choice cloze

 TIP: Be aware of what is being tested in each gap in Part 1.

Examples

Here are some examples of the different grammar and vocabulary points which can be tested in Part 1.

1. The four options may be similar in meaning, but only one is exactly right.

> Susan thinks it will take her more than a year to _____ enough money to buy a flat.
>
> **A** save ✓   **B** keep   **C** collect   **D** store

Explanation: The words are similar in meaning but only 'save' is used when you are putting money away until you have enough for a special purpose.

2. One of the four options may complete a set phrase such as 'pay attention'.

> I always _____ lots of photos when I go away on holiday.
>
> **A** make   **B** do   **C** put   **D** take ✓

Explanation: 'Take + photos' is a set phrase.

3. One of the four options completes a phrasal verb (or is the whole verb).

> It's my job to provide the raw material from which a natural history programme is _____ up.
>
> **A** made ✓   **B** set   **C** taken   **D** put

Explanation: You need a verb which means 'consists of' to complete the sentence, and only 'made + up' gives you this meaning.

Remember that phrasal verbs such as 'make up' can be tested in three different ways:
- the whole of the verb (make up)
- just the main part of the verb (make)
- the word following the main part of the verb (up).

4. The missing word is a linking word.

> There has been a change in people's attitudes towards the world. _____ people have been talking about global warming for many years, there is now great concern about its effects on the future of the planet.
>
> **A** Instead   **B** Whereas   **C** Although ✓ **D** However

Explanation: Read the sentence before and after the gap so that you understand exactly what the meaning is.

5. Sometimes the answer depends on the first word after the gap.

> Antonio was _____ of what would happen when his father discovered the truth.
>
> **A** afraid ✓ **B** concerned **C** worried   **D** anxious

Explanation: 'Afraid' is the only word that can be followed by 'of'.

Use of English: Part 2 open cloze

 TIP: Identify the kind of word that is being tested in each gap in Part 2.

Examples

Here are some examples of the different grammar and vocabulary points which can be tested in Part 2. The correct answer is in the sentence for you.

1. Pronouns and relative pronouns

> As soon as he saw the woman, the doctor realised that
> ...**her**... leg was broken.
> These are the houses ...**that/which**... are for sale.

2. Prepositions and set phrases

> I always try to study ...**in**... the morning when I am not tired.
> The expedition has so ...**far**... this year made more than 200
> dives into water 30 metres deep.

3. Phrasal verbs

> Large scale manufacturing has made it easier for young
> people to keep ...**up**... with changes in fashion.

4. Auxiliary verbs

> The two men ...**were**... seen in London last week walking
> along Oxford Street.

5. Conjunctions

> I took my umbrella ...**because/as**... it was raining when I
> left home.

6. Comparisons

> The weather was much colder on Sunday ...**than**... it had
> been on Saturday.

Other words often tested include articles (e.g. the), negatives (e.g. not), indefinites (e.g. any) and reference words (e.g. they).

Use of English: Part 2 open cloze

 TIP: You should read all of the sentence carefully before you decide what the missing word is. If you don't do this you may misunderstand and make a mistake.

Examples

1. Remember to read on to the end of the sentence which may be on the next line.

> Sarah had baked a banana cake for the first time and wondered _____ it would taste.

Explanation: In this example, the missing word would be 'how'.

> Sarah had baked a banana cake for the first time and wondered _____ it would taste like.

Explanation: In this example the missing word is 'what'.

2. You may also need to remember something earlier in the sentence.

> The girl felt very confident about doing well because she was making so _____ progress in her training.

Explanation: 'Confident' tells you that the missing word is positive and so the answer is 'much'.

> The girl felt very unsure about doing well because she was making so _____ progress in her training.

Explanation: 'Unsure' tells you that the missing word is negative and so the answer is 'little'.

Use of English: Part 3 word formation

TIP: You may need to make different sorts of changes to the words at the end of the line. Decide what kind of word you need (noun, verb, adjective, adverb) and then think about its form. Always check your spelling!

Example

Here is an example from a Part 3 text about working from home. The correct answers are in the gaps for you.

Working from home has become ❶ <u>increasingly</u> common as so many people own computers. Using email ❷ <u>enables</u> people to keep in touch with their offices on a regular ❸ <u>basis</u>, and many find it ❹ <u>enjoyable</u> to be able to work in the comfort of their own homes. Others find that the ❺ <u>length</u> of time they spend on their own during the working day can be rather lonely.

① INCREASE

② ABLE
③ BASE
④ ENJOY

⑤ LONG

Explanation: You may need to:

- add letters to the end of the word (suffix)
  e.g. CARE becomes careful (ly), careless (ly)

- add something to the front of the word (prefix)
  e.g. POSSIBLE becomes impossible

- make a change in the middle of the word
  e.g. STRONG becomes strength

- make more than one change to a word
  e.g. FORTUNATE becomes unfortunately.

Use of English: Part 3 word formation

 TIP: You should read the whole text carefully first to see what it is about, and to make it easier to see what kind of word is missing. You may need a negative or a plural. Make sure you read each full sentence (not just the line) before deciding on your answer.

Example

Here is an example from a Part 3 text about fame. The correct answers are in the gaps for you.

Would you like to be famous? Many people would, but they don't realise how many ➊disadvantages there are in living in the public eye. They are not prepared for the number of ➋photographers who hide round corners to take pictures of famous people at all hours of the day and night. Some ➌celebrities say that they would exchange their fame for a quiet life.

① ADVANTAGE

② PHOTOGRAPH

③ CELEBRITY

Explanation: The text tells you that living in the public eye is not a positive experience, so you know that ① must be negative ('**dis**advantage'). For ②, the preceding phrase ('the number of') and the following verb ('hide') mean that you need a plural word ('photographer**s**'). The verb 'say' requires a plural subject ③ after 'Some' in the last sentence, so you know that CELEBRITY must change to 'celebrit**ies**'.

Use of English Part 4 key word transformations

 TIP: Grammar and vocabulary are both tested, and there will always be two things you have to do in your answer.

Examples

Here are some examples (with answers) from Part 4.

> **1.** I haven't seen Sven for five years.
> **LAST**
> It's five years…**since I last saw**…Sven.

Explanation: 'since' + change of tense

> **2.** Cristina prefers films to plays.
> **LIKE**
> Cristina doesn't…**like plays as much as**…films.

Explanation: negative + comparison

> **3.** Jan is eager to see the film again next week.
> **LOOKING**
> Jan…**is looking forward to seeing**…the film again next week.

Explanation: paraphrase + 'to' and gerund

> **4.** Fortunately we had enough food at the party.
> **RUN**
> Fortunately, we…**didn't run out of**…food at the party.

Explanation: negative + phrasal verb

Use of English Part 4 key word transformations

TIP: Never write more than five words. If you do, you will get no marks. Don't add any words that are unnecessary because you might change the meaning of the sentence as well as write too many words.

Examples

Here are some examples of Part 4 questions.

1. I was really bored by the lecture.
   FOUND
   I…**found the lecture really**…boring. ✓

2. Claire failed to persuade Sylvie to come on holiday with us.
   SUCCEED
   Claire did not…**really succeed at all in persuading**… Sylvie to come on holiday with us. ✗

Explanation: If you remove 'really' and 'at all', this sentence would be correct.

3. We didn't go to the cinema because John was ill.
   IF
   We would have gone to the cinema…**if John hadn't been very**…ill. ✗

Explanation: If you remove 'very', this sentence would be correct.

4. 'I'm sorry I held the meeting up yesterday', Jenny said.
   APOLOGISED
   Jenny…**apologised for having held/apologised for holding**…the meeting up the previous day. ✓

Contractions count as two words, apart from 'can't' which can be written as one word (cannot).

General tips for Use of English

1 In the exam, check that all your spellings are correct, and that your writing is clear and easy to read. Spelling must be correct all through the paper.

2 Use your dictionary when preparing for the exam (although you can't use it in the exam itself). A good monolingual dictionary will help you to find new collocations and new ways of using familiar words.

3 When you come across a new word, write down all its forms (noun, verb, adjective, adverb) and any collocations. Remember that one word can have more than one meaning and use.

4 Sometimes there may be more than one possible answer for a gap. Only write one on the answer sheet. If you write two answers and they are both correct, you will get the mark, but if you write two answers and one is wrong, you will not.

5 Read the texts in **Parts 1, 2 and 3** through with the missing words added to make sure they make sense.

6 Check that you have not made any silly mistakes such as misspelling the given word in **Part 4**.

 NOW YOU TRY! You will find a complete Use of English paper (and answer sheet) to try on the CD-ROM. Give yourself 45 minutes to work through the whole paper.

When you have finished you can check your answers.

Paper 4: Listening

What's in the Listening paper?

Part 1 ⓠ 8 short listening texts with 1 multiple-choice question for each

☑ 1 mark for each correct answer

Part 2 ⓠ a longer listening text with 10 sentence-completion questions

☑ 1 mark for each correct answer

Part 3 ⓠ 5 short listening texts to match to a series of statements

☑ 1 mark for each correct answer

Part 4 ⓠ a longer listening text with 7 multiple-choice questions

☑ 1 mark for each correct answer

🕐 Approximately **40 minutes**
(including 5 minutes to copy your answers onto the answer sheet)

Listening Part 1 multiple choice

TIP: Underline the key words in the question. All the possible answers may be mentioned in the recording, but only one will actually **answer the question**. Then listen for words which mean the same as the key words. These will tell you that the correct answer is coming.

Example

Here is a question from a Part 1 task about a man with an interesting job, together with part of the tapescript.

 Q **What made him leave the job?**
  A His family wanted him to
  B He needed more job security ✓
  C He had a number of accidents

TAPESCRIPT

I was what is called a 'base' jumper – somebody who jumps from tall buildings and bridges. I worked for film companies or photographers … I loved it … There's a big difference between that and my present job as a ski instructor. It was a difficult decision, giving up jumping, but I felt I needed a good regular income. A lot of people thought I'd just had enough of doing a dangerous job. And my wife had asked me to stop. But not even having children made me question whether I should carry on. Accidents didn't put me off either. I broke my ankle twice and once I even broke a rib but I still felt I wanted to …

Explanation: 'Leave' in the question refers to 'giving up' (jumping) when you listen to the recording. This introduces the answer. 'I felt I needed a good regular income' tells us that the man needed a more secure job, so the answer is **B**.

Listening Part 1 multiple choice

 TIP: In a dialogue, make sure that you listen for the right person. All the options may be mentioned, but not necessarily by **the person in the question**. You may have to listen for this person's attitude or opinion, which may not be a single word or phrase.

Example

Here is a question from a Part 1 task about a trip to the cinema. You hear two people talking about a film they've just seen.

 What did <u>the man dislike</u> about it?

    A the plot ✓

    B the actors

    C the length

TAPESCRIPT

WOMAN: So you weren't very impressed with the film then? I must say three hours did seem a bit too much but the acting was terrific, didn't you think?

MAN: I'd made up my mind about it after the first half hour.

WOMAN: What do you mean?

MAN: Well, I thought the storyline was just too difficult to follow.

WOMAN: Did you? I don't know about that. But the performers were good, weren't they?

MAN: But that's not enough, is it? I mean the performers have to have a good script to work with and that's where I felt …

Explanation: The woman talks about the actors and the length of the film, but the man says all the way through that he didn't like the storyline ('plot') so his attitude is one of *dislike*. The answer is therefore **A**.

Listening Part 2 sentence completion

TIP: Read all the sentences through **before** you listen and think about the meaning of each one. Remember that you may not hear the exact words in the sentences in the recording, but you do have to write the exact word or phrase you hear spoken and nothing else.

Examples

Here are some sentences from a Part 2 task about a woman sailor, together with the parts of the tapescript where you can find the answers.

> The sailors in Stella's crew are <u>all</u> ❶ ...**women**...

 One of the things people want to know is whether having only women in your crew makes any difference?

> The food on the boat doesn't taste nice because it is all ❷ ...**dried**...

 And all our cooking is done in a very small space below deck. That's a horrible job, especially in rough seas as you get to feel very sick if you are stuck below deck! And the food tastes disgusting anyway – everything is dried so it doesn't go bad and doesn't weigh much or take up a lot of space.

> The use of the colours ❸ ...**blue**... and ❹ ...**yellow**... make the boat and sails easily recognisable.

 You'll see our boat easily when the races are on television! It looks really beautiful because although it was a dirty brown colour when we bought it, it's now been repainted in blue to contrast with the yellow sails we use in preference to white or red.

If you have two items (e.g. 'blue' and 'yellow'), remember that you can put them in either order.

Listening Part 2 sentence completion

TIP: Be aware that you may hear more than one piece of information that could fit the gap. For example, you may hear several numbers or months in the recording, but you must make sure you choose the correct one to fill the gap.

Examples

Here are some sentences from a Part 2 task about a woman sailor, together with the part of the tapescript where you can find the answers.

Stella will begin the Round-the-World race in the month of **5** **...December...**

TAPESCRIPT

Well, we're not all that keen on just doing meaningless training. We look on one race as training for the next! So in September we'll be sailing across the Atlantic. We'll begin in New York and race to Plymouth in south-west England. After that, we'll be spending the months of October and November getting into shape for our biggest test so far – that's the Round-the-World race which we'll start in early December from the Bay of Biscay.

Explanation: Although you hear four months (September, October, November and December) in the recording, the Round-the-World race will start in December.

To break the record, Stella has to sail around the world in less than **6** **...71...** days.

We're really hopeful that we can do better than the existing record, which means doing it in under 71 days. Although no-one's managed it in less than 75 days for a number of years now.

Explanation: Stella mentions two numbers ('71 days' and '75 days'), but 71 days is the record she has to break.

Listening Part 3 multiple matching

 TIP: When you read the question, try to think of other ways of saying it. You will hear words which mean the same on the recording, so this will help you to identify the speaker.

Examples

Here are some questions from Part 3 texts about jobs, and the part of the tapescript where you can find the answers.

1.

 Q People trust me not to spend too much money on a project.

 TAPESCRIPT

SPEAKER 1: TELEVISION PRODUCER

Whatever stage of production it is, the battle is always the same, it's a fight against time and costs – and knowing what can be done within those limits. I've got a reputation for finishing things on time and at a reasonable cost – and it's a reputation I couldn't afford to lose.

Explanation: The question sentence means 'I keep costs down/I don't spend a lot of money/My projects are cheap'. This matches what Speaker 1 says (highlighted in the tapescript).

2.

 I could lose my job if my ideas don't make money for the company.

TAPESCRIPT

SPEAKER 2: WORKS FOR A PRODUCT DEVELOPMENT AGENCY

Everyone in our company knows we have to do well and make money. If someone isn't giving the customers what they want, then they have to go. Five people were dismissed recently, so the rest of us feel rather insecure, but all the more determined to come up with successful new products.

Explanation: You could rewrite the question sentence as 'I could get the sack/I might be dismissed/I could go'. This matches what Speaker 2 says (highlighted in the tapescript).

On the first listening, don't be nervous if you have not got all the answers. Only fill in the answers you are absolutely sure of, and use the second listening to confirm your ideas.

Listening Part 4 multiple choice

 TIP: The **first** time you listen, try to identify the correct answer. The **second** time you listen, confirm your answer by working out why the others are wrong.

Example

Here is a question from a Part 4 task about a famous mystery and the part of the tapescript where you can find the answer.

> **Q** **When the mystery started, William Homes**
>
> **A** was working for a village shoemaker
>
> **B** was living and working in a small village ✓
>
> **C** had just bought his own workshop

TAPESCRIPT

SUE: And it all happened in your part of the world, didn't it?

HENRY: That's right – a small village quite near where I was born. A young shoemaker called William Homes had rented a small house and workshop in the village and was living and working there alone. It was soon after he set up the business, in 1825, that he began to be troubled by this really strange series of events.

Explanation:

A is wrong because William was the shoemaker himself. ✗

C is wrong because William rented the workshop. ✗

The highlighted words in the tapescript show you that the correct answer is **B**. ✓

Listening Part 4 multiple choice

 TIP: Read through the questions and options and underline key words. This will help you to focus on the important information.

Example

Here is a question from a Part 4 task about a famous mystery, and the part of the tapescript where you can find the answer.

 What does the man say <u>surprised</u> Homes about the tin?

A It had not been opened.

B It had had something put in it. ✓

C It had been moved to a different place.

TAPESCRIPT

HENRY: Well, the whole thing was later reported in the local paper. Apparently Homes used to keep his glue in a tin in the workshop, but one morning he noticed the tin, which he'd left empty the night before, was filled with little bits of leather and other things.

SUE: Uh huh ...

HENRY: And this soon began to happen on a regular basis. Every time it did, he noticed that some long strips of leather had been laid over the tin in the shape of a star, which he found really strange.

SUE: And Homes wondered who could be doing it?

Explanation:

A is wrong because the tin was empty, but had been filled. ✗

C is wrong because there is no information to tell us that the tin had been moved. ✗

The highlighted words in the tapescript show you that the correct answer is B. ✓

General tips for Listening

1 Use the time you have to read through the questions so that you know exactly what you are listening for.

2 You hear the instructions on the recording. Always listen carefully and read the question at the same time, as they give you the context and the topic.

3 If you are not sure of an answer, mark those that you think are possible. Use the second listening to confirm your choice.

4 Use the second listening to check your answer even if you are sure you are right. Don't stop listening!

5 Make sure you write clearly when transferring your answers to the answer sheet. You have plenty of time to do this.

6 Write only the missing word or short phrase on the answer sheet in **Part 2,** and don't rephrase it.

7 Don't choose an answer based on a single word or phrase in **Parts 1, 3** and **4** – concentrate on the overall meaning of what you hear.

 NOW YOU TRY! You will find a complete Listening paper (with an answer sheet) to try on the CD-ROM, as well as all the recordings you need. Give yourself 40 minutes to work through the whole paper.

When you have finished you can check your answers.

Paper 5: Speaking

What's in the Speaking test?

Part 1 ⓠ conversation with the examiner in which you give personal information and opinions

Part 2 ⓠ you compare 2 photographs and answer a question

Part 3 ⓠ you discuss some pictures with the other candidate and reach a decision

Part 4 ⓠ further discussion about the task from Part 3

🕐 **14 minutes** *per pair of candidates*

Your speaking is assessed on:
- grammar and vocabulary
- discourse management (i.e. the development of ideas)
- pronunciation
- interactive communication
- global achievement

Speaking Part 1 interview

TIP: Don't just answer 'yes' or 'no' to the interlocutor's questions; try to explain 'why'. The interlocutor may ask you 'why?', but it is better if you can give the reason yourself. The questions ask you about yourself, so you should include personal details to make your answer interesting.

Examples

1.

INTERLOCUTOR:	What do you like about living in your country?
CANDIDATE:	I like the weather as it's always warm and sunny and I can go out with my friend to the beach. I love that!

2.

INTERLOCUTOR:	Do you like going to parties?
CANDIDATE:	I love going out with my friends but I'm not so keen on parties because they are always so noisy and it's difficult to talk. I prefer meeting my friends in a restaurant so that we can have a nice meal and time to talk.

3.

INTERLOCUTOR:	What kind of work would you like to do in the future?
CANDIDATE:	At the moment I'm a student so I don't work but in the future I would like to become a chef. I love cooking and that's why I think it would be very interesting to have my own restaurant.

Explanation: The examples above all give reasons. Look at the highlighted words.

4.

INTERLOCUTOR:	Do you use the internet to learn new things?
CANDIDATE:	Oh yes, I use the internet all the time – I send emails to my friends and I also use it to find out information. And last week I saw a really good television programme about dolphins and then I looked up more information about them on the internet. It was really interesting!

5.

INTERLOCUTOR:	Are you happier doing mental or physical work?
CANDIDATE:	Well, I'm not really much good at physical work – I don't think I'm very strong and I hate going to the gym. I like reading or doing something like a crossword or that numbers game – I think it's called Su duko or something like that. I did one of those really quickly last week and my friends couldn't believe it!

Explanation: Examples 4 and 5 show answers where the candidate has added more information and personal details.

Speaking Part 2 long turn

 TIP: The task is written on the paper with the pictures, so use this to remind yourself of what you have to talk about. There are always **two** parts to the task, so divide your talk into two sections to make sure that you cover both parts.

Example

Here is an example of a Part 2 Speaking task.

INTERLOCUTOR: Here are your photographs. They show people sightseeing in different places.

INTERLOCUTOR: I'd like you to compare the photographs, and say what you think the people are enjoying about sightseeing in these different places.

CANDIDATE:

COMPARE

In both pictures I can see some tourists, but they are doing different things. In the first picture they're just about to go sightseeing on a tourist boat. They're sitting in the boat waiting for the tour to start. However, in the second picture I can see some tourists going sightseeing on foot, not in a boat. I think they're probably walking up the Great Wall of China, so that's much more energetic.

WHAT YOU THINK

I think both groups of tourists are enjoying themselves, but maybe for different reasons. I think the first group will enjoy seeing the town from the water because it looks different when you see it this way and it's very relaxing. It's much nicer than walking around a town with crowds of other tourists on a hot day. Often when you go on boats like this one there's a guide who gives you lots of information about the town and that can be very interesting. In the second picture it's not so relaxing for the tourists – it's probably a hot day because they do look quite tired. But it must be a great experience for them to be there – I think everyone would enjoy going to see something so special.

Explanation: The example above shows how a good candidate might address both parts of the question. The highlighted words in the first paragraph of the answer show you some language you can use to compare the pictures.

Speaking Part 2 long turn

 TIP: Listen while your partner is speaking, because you have to give a short answer to a question about their photographs when they have finished. Do **not** interrupt while your partner is speaking!

Example

Here is an example of a question which the listening candidate had to answer in Part 2. You can find the pictures on p. 50.

INTERLOCUTOR:	Which place would you prefer to go to?
CANDIDATE:	I think I'd prefer to go to China, because I'd like to find out more about the life there, and this picture looks very interesting.

Explanation: The answer above is a good answer because it provides enough relevant language to respond and is not too long. Remember that you should not say too much about your partner's pictures in your answer, because you will be given two different photographs to talk about. You only have to speak for about 20 seconds.

Speaking Part 3 collaborative task

 TIP: The task has two parts, but the first part is the most important. Say as much as you can about each picture. The task is written on the page with the pictures to remind you of what to talk about.

Example

In this example of a Part 3 task about public transport, you have to imagine that the government is producing a poster to encourage people to use public transport. You can find the pictures on pp. 54–55.

INTERLOCUTOR:	First talk to each other about why these ideas might encourage people to use public transport. Then decide which two photographs they should use for the poster.
CANDIDATE A:	Shall we start with this picture – a train? And it looks like a fast one, so that would be good because you'd get to your destination very quickly – better than a car.
CANDIDATE B:	I agree. And the picture below shows how bad the cars are for the environment.
CANDIDATE A:	And look at this picture in the top right – a traffic jam. If you saw that on a poster, you'd remember how difficult it is to travel by car in a city.
CANDIDATE B:	You're right – it's so slow and people get very irritated, don't they?
CANDIDATE A:	Let's look at the picture below. The woman's working on the train and she looks very relaxed. That would encourage business people to go by train.
CANDIDATE B:	We haven't talked about this picture yet …

Explanation: The highlighted words show the language which you might use to discuss each picture. When you practise Part 3, go through the pictures in turn with your partner.

Speaking Part 3 collaborative task

 TIP: Interact with your partner as you talk about each picture. Use different strategies during your discussion – don't just ask your partner questions. Listen to what they say, and respond by agreeing, disagreeing or making another suggestion. Take turns, and don't dominate the conversation.

Example

Here is an example from Part 3. The candidates had to imagine that the government is producing a poster to encourage people to use public transport. They had to discuss some photographs (on pp. 54–55) and then decide which two photographs to use for the poster.

CANDIDATE A:	What do you think about the idea of having high speed trains? That would make it quicker for people to get around and it's much better for the environment than cars!
CANDIDATE B:	I agree with you, but tickets might be very expensive and so that might discourage people. I like trains myself, but some people feel ill on them! You said that it would be quicker to get around – what do you think about the idea of buses? They are often not as expensive as trains, and this picture seems to show someone cleaning a bus, and so maybe they are going to have clean, comfortable buses.
CANDIDATE A:	You're right – maybe it's suggesting that the buses are pleasant to travel on, and in my country buses are always cheaper than trains. And I agree with what you said about buses being cheaper.

Explanation: The highlighted words in the candidate answers above show good examples of interacting with a partner.

Speaking Part 4 discussion

 TIP: Listen to what your partner says and then agree, disagree or add more detail. Be sensitive. Don't talk for too long without giving your partner a chance to speak.

Example

Here is an example of a discussion from Part 4 of a Speaking test.

INTERLOCUTOR:	**What do you think could be done to improve public transport in this area?**
CANDIDATE A:	Well, first of all, we need more buses. Don't you think so?
CANDIDATE B:	Absolutely, and not just more buses, but buses that run on time.
CANDIDATE A:	I agree. If the buses were better, then people would use them.
CANDIDATE B:	And another thing, a lot are quite old and a bit dirty, so newer buses would be good. And what do you think about the train service in this area?

Explanation: The highlighted words show the language candidates use to agree and add more detail.

 *Always say something, and have an opinion! It doesn't matter if it is right or wrong – you are being assessed on your language, not your ideas.*

General tips for Speaking

1 Don't worry if the interlocutor stops you before you have finished everything that you want to say. You and your partner will be given the exact time set out in the test.

2 Always speak clearly so that the assessor and the interlocutor can hear you.

3 Don't worry if you make a grammatical mistake – that is only part of the assessment.

4 Don't prepare sentences or short speeches before the test. React to what the interlocutor and your partner say to you.

5 In **Part 2** and **Part 3**, remember that the task is written at the top of the page, but if you aren't sure what to do, ask the interlocutor to repeat the instructions before you start. You can also check what you have to do with your partner.

6 Don't try to talk all the time. Don't interrupt your partner while they are speaking – wait until they have finished.

7 Relax and try not to be nervous – enjoy the experience!

 NOW YOU TRY! You will find a complete Speaking test on the CD-ROM, together with the pictures and the script for the interlocutor. Practise with a partner, and you will feel more confident when you take the test.

What to do on the day

Very few people like taking exams, but you can make the day of the exam easier if you make sure you know what to expect and what you will have to do before you go to the exam centre or place where you take your FCE exam.

Rules and regulations

For any exam you take, there are some rules and regulations about what you **must** do and what you **mustn't** do during the exam. Read through the Cambridge ESOL rules and regulations below and if there is anything you don't understand, ask your teacher. On the day of the exam, you can also ask the examination supervisor if you are not sure.

You must ...

- provide a valid photographic proof of your identity (for example: national identity card, passport, college ID or driving licence) and your Statement of Entry for each paper you take
- only have on your desk what you need to complete the examination (pens, pencils and erasers)
- switch off your mobile phone and any other electronic device (the supervisor will tell you where you have to put them)
- stop writing immediately when you are told to do so.

You must not ...

- cheat, copy, give anything to another candidate, take anything from another candidate, or break any of the rules during the examination
- have with you any electronic device (this includes mobile phones)
- use, or attempt to use, a dictionary
- use correction fluid on the answer sheets
- talk to or disturb other candidates during the examination
- smoke or eat in the examination room. However, you are allowed to drink plain, still water from a plastic bottle with a secure lid.

Advice and information

We hope that all our candidates will have a positive experience of taking a Cambridge ESOL exam. So, we have prepared some advice and information so that you know what to do if there are any problems on the day that you take your exam. Make sure that you have read and understand all the information and advice below before you go into the exam.

Make sure you are on time

- Know the date, time and place of your examination and arrive well before the start time.
- If you arrive late for any part of the examination, report to the supervisor or invigilator. You may not be allowed to take the examination. Also, if you are admitted, not all of your work may be accepted.
- If you miss any part of the examination, you will not normally be given a grade.

Instructions for taking the test

- The supervisor will tell you what you have to do. The instructions are also written on the question paper and the answer sheet.
- Listen to the supervisor and read the instructions carefully.
- Tell the supervisor or invigilator at once if you think you have the wrong question paper, or if the question paper is incomplete or badly printed.

Advice and assistance during the examination

- If you are not sure about what to do, raise your hand to attract attention. The invigilator will come to help you.
- You must not ask for, and will not be given, any explanation of the questions.
- If you do not feel well on the day of the examination or think that your work may be affected for any other reason, tell the supervisor or invigilator.

Leaving the examination room

- Do not leave the examination room for any reason without the permission of the supervisor or invigilator.
- The supervisor will tell you when you can and can't leave the room.
- You must wait until the supervisor has collected your question paper, answer sheet(s) and any paper used for rough work before you leave the examination room.
- You must not take any information relating to the examination questions or answers out of the examination room.
- Do not make any noise near the examination room.

Answer sheets

On the day you take the exam, you can write on the question paper while you decide what the correct answer is. However, when you have made a decision, you **must** transfer your final answers onto the candidate answer sheets which the supervisor will give you for the Reading, Use of English and Listening papers.

How to complete the answer sheets

You can see an example of what an answer sheet looks like on the next page and practise using them when you try the papers on the CD-ROM. There are instructions on the answer sheets to tell you how you should fill them in, but here are the main things you need to know:

- It is very important that you use a **pencil** to write your answers on the answer sheets. (We use a special machine to check some of your answers and it can only 'see' pencil marks.)
- Where you have to choose an answer (A, B, C or D, etc.), you must make a clear pencil mark inside the box you choose. Don't, for example, put a circle around the box, because the machine won't 'see' this.
- If you have to write a word or phrase for your answer, please write clearly. If the examiners can't read your writing, they won't know if your answer is correct or not.
- If you change your mind about an answer, it is important that you use an eraser to rub out the answer you don't want.

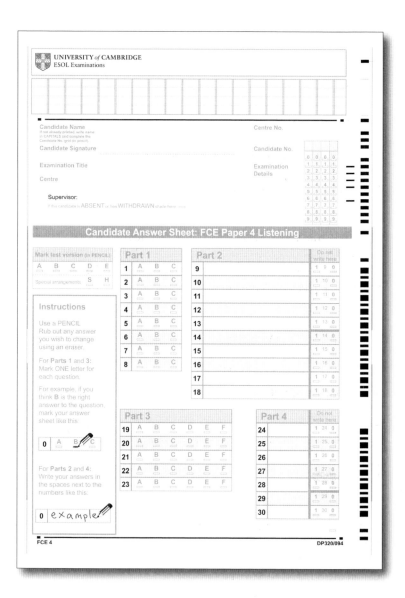

What next after FCE?

We hope that you will enjoy studying for FCE and that you will be successful when you take the exam. A Cambridge ESOL qualification is a great achievement and you can be proud of your result.

When you receive your results and certificate, you will probably start to think about what you can do next to continue to improve your English, so here are some suggestions:

Using FCE for work or study

All around the world, FCE is the Cambridge ESOL exam which most people take. Many companies and educational institutions in many different countries recognise FCE as proof of your level of English when you are looking for a job or applying for a place to study.

For the future, you may be thinking about studying abroad or working in a company where you need to use your English. If this is something which interests you, have a look at the Recognition database on the Cambridge ESOL website:

www.CambridgeESOL.org/recognition/search.php

Search the database for the specific information you need about how and where you can use FCE. Using the information in the database, you can find out about the many possibilities, both for work and further study, which are open to you when you pass FCE.

Taking the next Cambridge ESOL exam

If you are thinking of continuing your English studies, the next level of the Cambridge ESOL exams for you is the Certificate in Advanced English (CAE). You can find more information about CAE on our Candidate Support website at:

www.candidates.CambridgeESOL.org

How to use the CD-ROM

'Now you try!' at the end of each of the main sections of *Top Tips for FCE* is your chance to try a real exam paper and you will find these on the CD-ROM.

Insert the CD into the CD drive on your computer. (On some Windows PC computers the application will launch automatically; if it does not you will need to launch it by double-clicking the application icon named 'FCE_TopTips'.) Once the application starts, simply follow the instructions on screen.

To open and print the exam papers (pdf documents)

On a PC

The exam papers are in pdf format, so if you are using a Windows PC, you need to install and set Adobe Reader as the default pdf viewer in order to open and print them. You can download Adobe Reader free from: **www.adobe.com**

On a Mac

Apple Mac computers with OSX will be able to open and print the pdf files using the built-in Apple Preview application.

If you have any difficulties opening the pdf files from the CD interface, you can find them in a folder called 'pdf_documents' by exploring the CD's contents. You will then be able to open and print them manually using a pdf viewing application.

System requirements

For PC

Essential:	Windows 2000, XP or Vista, CD Drive & Audio capabilities
Recommended:	400 MHz processor or faster, with 256mb of RAM or more

For Mac

Essential:	Mac OSX, version 10.3 or higher
Recommended:	400 MHz G3 processor or faster, with 256mb of RAM or more